A Friendship Gift, a title in the Tiny Tea series
© 2001 by Dee Appel
Published by Blue Cottage Gifts™, a division of Multnomah Publishers, Inc.
P.O. Box 1720, Sisters, OR 97759

ISBN 1-58860-027-0

Artwork by Gay Talbott Boassy
All works of art reproduced in this book are copyrighted by Gay Talbott Boassy and
may not be reproduced without the artist's permission. For more information regarding
art featured in this book, please contact:

       Mr. Gifford B. Bowne II
       Indigo Gate, Inc.
       1 Pegasus Drive
       Colts Neck, NJ 07722
       (732) 577-9333

Designed by Koechel Peterson & Associates, Minneapolis, Minnesota

Scripture quotation taken from *The Holy Bible*, New King James Version (NKJV)
©1984 by Thomas Nelson, Inc.

Printed in China

01 02 03 04 05 06 — 10 9 8 7 6 5 4 3 2 1 0
www.bluecottagegifts.com

A Friendship Gift

TEXT BY DEE APPEL   ART BY GAY TALBOTT BOASSY

BLUE COTTAGE GIFTS™

a division of Multnomah Publishers, Inc.
Sisters, Oregon

I'm sending you this little gift;
it's just for you from me.
So take a little time today
to have a Tiny Tea.

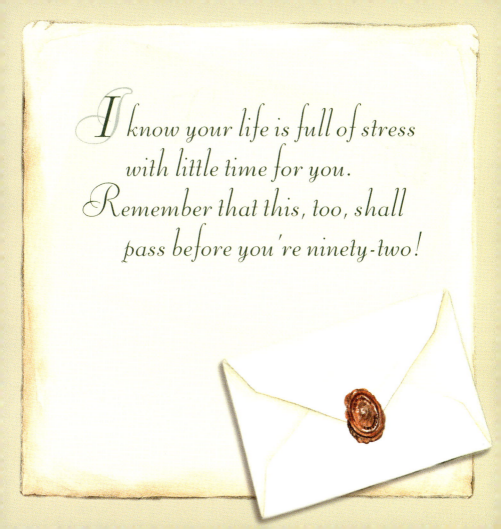

I know your life is full of stress with little time for you. Remember that this, too, shall pass before you're ninety-two!

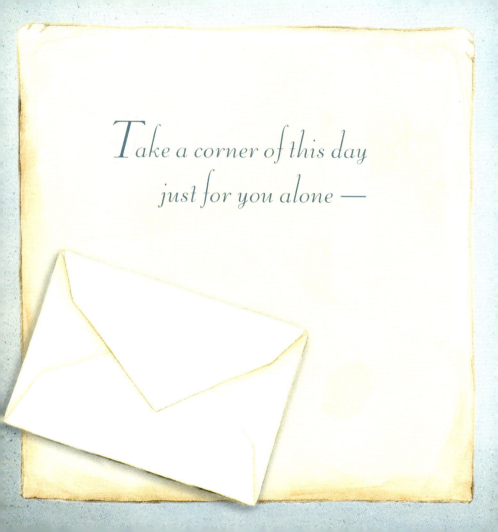

*T*ake a corner of this day
just for you alone —

Lock the door, pull the shades, and disconnect the phone.

Fill the tub up to its brim and bathe by candles' glow. Remember you are loved a lot, in case you didn't know.

Then brew yourself a cup of tea,
release a sigh or two.
You'll find that things are not so
bad when you take time for you.

*Think back to days
of backyard teas
when guests were
dolls and friends,*

And for a moment sweet
recall how simple life was then.

And when your life
returns to "norm,"

I hope you'll think of me,

*And capture brief
that soft, sweet break,
when you had a Tiny Tea.*

*O*intment and perfume
delight the heart,
*A*nd the sweetness of a
man's friend gives delight...

Proverbs 27:9